KIDS' TRAVEL GUIDE LONDON

FlyingKids PRESENTS:

KIDS' TRAVEL GUIDE

LONDON

Author: Sara-Jane Williams
Editor: Carma Graber
Graphic designer: Francesca Guido
Published by FlyingKids Limited

Visit us @ **www.theflyingkids.com**
Contact us: **leonardo@theflyingkids.com**

ISBN: 978-1-910994-16-0

Table of Contents

This is the only page for parents in this book ... 😉

Dear Parents,

If you bought this book, you're probably planning a family trip with your kids.
You are spending a lot of time and money in the hopes that this family vacation will be pleasant and fun. Of course, you would be happy for your **children** to get to know the city you are visiting—a little about its geography, **local history**, important sites, **culture**, customs, and more. And you hope they will always remember the trip as a very special **experience**.
The reality is often quite different. Parents find themselves **frustrated** as they struggle to convince their kids to join a tour or visit a landmark, while the kids just want to stay in and watch TV—or they're glued to their mobile devices and take in very little of the new sights and experiences. Many parents are **disappointed** after they return home and discover that their **kids don't remember** much about the trip and the new things they learned.
That's exactly why the Kids' Travel Guides were created.
With the Kids' Travel Guides, young children become **researchers** and **active participants** in the trip. The Kids' Travel Guides include **puzzles**, **tasks** to complete, useful **tips**, and other recommendations along the way. During the vacation, kids will read relevant facts about the city you are visiting. They will meet *Leonardo—their very own tour guide*. Leonardo encourages them to experiment, explore, and be more **involved in the family's activities**—as well as to learn new information and make memories throughout the trip. In addition, kids are encouraged to document and write about their experiences, so that when you return home, they will have a memoir that will be fun to look at and reread again and again The Kids' Travel Guides support children as they **get ready** for the trip, **visit** new places, **learn** new things, and finally, return **home**.
The *Kids' Travel Guide—London* focuses on the city nicknamed "The Smoke"! In it, children will find **background information** on **London** and its special attractions. The *Kids' Travel Guide—London* focuses on **central sites** that are recommended for children. At each of these sites, interesting blurbs, **action items**, and **quizzes** await your kids.
You, the parents, are invited to participate or to find an available bench and relax while you enjoy your **active** children.
If you are traveling to **London**, you may also want to get the *Kids' Travel Guide—United Kingdom*, which focuses **on the countries of the UK**—their geography, history, unique culture, traditions, and more—all in the fun and interesting style of the Kids' Travel Guide series.

READY FOR A NEW EXPERIENCE?

Have a nice trip and have fun!

Hi, Kids!

If you are reading this book, it means you are lucky—you are going to **London**!

You may have noticed that your parents are getting ready for the journey. They have bought travel guides, looked for information on the Internet, and printed pages of information. They are talking to friends and people who have already visited London in order to learn about it and know what to do, where to go, and when ...

But this book is not just another guidebook for your parents.
This book is for you only—the young traveler.

First and foremost, meet Leonardo, your very own personal guide on this trip. Leonardo has visited many places around the world. (Guess how he got there?)
He will be with you throughout the book and the trip. Leonardo will tell you all about the places you will visit—it is always good to learn a little bit about the city and its history beforehand.
Leonardo will provide many ideas, quizzes, tips, and other surprises. He will be with you while you are packing and leaving home, and he will stay in the hotel with you (don't worry, it does not cost more money)!
And he will see the sights with you until you return home.

HAVE FUN!

THE BEGINNING!

GOING TO LONDON!!!

How did you get to London?

By plane / ship / car / train / other ______________

Date of arrival ________ Time ________ Date of departure ________

All in all, we will stay in London for ______ days.

Is this your first visit ? ______________

Where will you sleep? In a hotel / in a motel /
in an apartment / with family / in a guesthouse / other ______________

What sites are you planning to visit?

____

____

____

What special activities are you planning to do?

____

____

____

Are you excited about the trip?

This is an excitement indicator. Ask your family members how excited they are (from "not at all" up to "very, very much"), and mark each of their answers on the indicator. Leonardo has already marked the level of his excitement ...

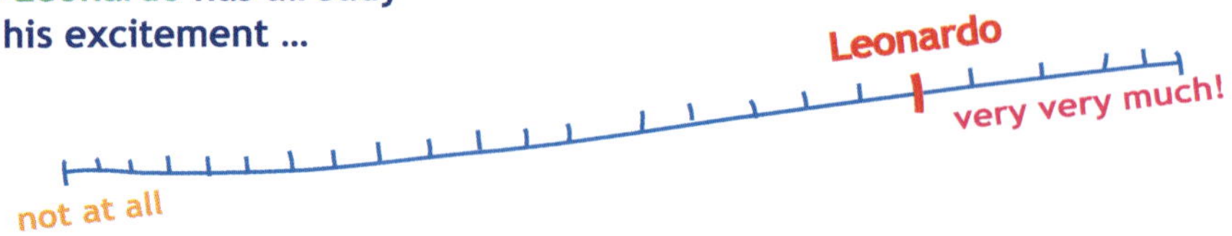

Who is traveling?

Write down the names of family members traveling with you.

Name: ____________

Age: ____________

Has he or she visited London before? yes / no

What is the most exciting thing about your upcoming trip?

____

____

____

Name: ____________

Age: ____________

Has he or she visited London before? yes / no

What is the most exciting thing about your upcoming trip?

____

____

____

Name: ____________

Age: ____________

Has he or she visited London before? yes / no

What is the most exciting thing about your upcoming trip?

____

____

____

Name: ____________

Age: ____________

Has he or she visited London before? yes / no

What is the most exciting thing about your upcoming trip?

____

____

____

Name: ____________

Age: ____________

Has he or she visited London before? yes / no

What is the most exciting thing about your upcoming trip?

____

____

____

Paste a picture of your family.

Preparations at home – do not forget ...!

Mom or Dad will take care of packing clothes (how many pairs of pants, which comb to take ...). So Leonardo will only tell you about the things he thinks you may want to bring along to London.

Here's the **Packing List** Leonardo made for you. You can check off each item as you pack it:

- [x] *Kids' Travel Guide—London*—of course!
- [ ] Comfortable walking shoes
- [ ] A raincoat (One that folds up is best—sometimes it rains without warning ...)
- [ ] A hat (and sunglasses, if you want)
- [ ] Pens and pencils
- [ ] Crayons and markers (It is always nice to color and paint.)
- [ ] A notebook or writing pad (You can use it for games or writing, or to draw or doodle in when you're bored ...)
- [ ] A book to read
- [ ] Your smartphone/tablet or camera
- [ ] ____________________
- [ ] ____________________

TIPS!

Pack your things in a small bag (or **backpack**). You may also want to take these things:

- ☐ Snacks, fruit, candy, and chewing gum. If you are flying, it can help a lot during takeoff and landing, when there's pressure in your ears.
- ☐ Games you can play while sitting down: electronic games, booklets of crossword puzzles, connect-the-numbers (or connect-the-dots), etc.

Now let's see if you can find 12 items you should take on a trip in this word search puzzle:

- ☐ Leonardo
- ☐ walking shoes
- ☐ hat
- ☐ raincoat
- ☐ crayons
- ☐ book
- ☐ pencil
- ☐ camera
- ☐ snacks
- ☐ fruit
- ☐ patience
- ☐ good mood

P	A	T	I	E	N	C	E	A	W	F	G
E	L	R	T	S	G	Y	J	W	A	T	O
Q	E	Y	U	Y	K	Z	K	M	L	W	O
H	O	S	N	A	S	N	Y	S	K	G	D
A	N	R	Z	C	P	E	N	C	I	L	M
C	A	M	E	R	A	A	W	G	N	E	O
R	R	A	I	N	C	O	A	T	G	Q	O
Y	D	S	G	I	R	K	Z	K	S	H	D
S	O	A	C	O	A	E	T	K	H	A	T
F	R	U	I	T	Y	Q	O	V	O	D	A
B	O	O	K	F	O	H	Z	K	E	R	T
T	K	Z	K	A	N	S	I	E	S	Y	U
O	V	I	E	S	S	N	A	C	K	S	P

WELCOME TO LONDON !!!

London is a lively and exciting city with so much to see and do! It's the **capital city** of both England and the whole United Kingdom (UK). London is located in the southern part of England. You'll see the River Thames running through the city. The Thames is the second longest river in the UK.

London has had a few nicknames over the years—the most popular is **"The Smoke,"** or sometimes **"The Big Smoke."** That's because Londoners used to heat their homes by burning coal—and the city also had lots of factories—so the air was very smoky! Sometimes it was hard to breathe.

In the 1960s, London was often called **"The Swinging City."** It was the center of "mod" fashion and popular music.

London is a very **multicultural and multinational** city. This means that people from lots of different nations, with lots of different cultures, live in the city. Some of the different groups have been living in London for many years—and new people are still coming to the city from all over the world.

London is now home to around **9 million** people!

What is the capital city of your country?

____

Does it have a nickname?

____

Do any major rivers flow through your country's capital city?

____

What is the main language in your country?

____

London city map

Greater London is HUGE! It is divided into several different areas that are called **boroughs**. A borough is like a small town or district—it's a smaller piece of the whole area. There are 32 London boroughs, plus the City of London.

The main tourist spots can be found in the central part of the city, although there are plenty of great things to do in the outer areas too!

What places are you really looking forward to seeing in London?

____

____

____

Did you know?

A major highway—the M25—runs all around the edge of Greater London. The M25 is often called the London Orbital, because of the way it seems to orbit around the city!

The historic heart of London is the old City of London. The old city is actually the smallest city in the UK! It is often called the "Square Mile."

Can you guess why?!

Answer: The old City of London is just around one square mile in size!

Can you circle them on the map?

Can you also put a star where your hotel is?

London's very long history

Who built London?

The old City of London was built by **Romans** who invaded Britain. It was a really small city back then ... The Romans called it **"Londinium."**

A city destroyed

An army led by a British queen named Boudica forced the Romans out of London. Then Boudica had the city **burned down**! But the Romans came back and rebuilt London, adding a wall around it for protection. They left in the fifth century.

French invasions and hard lives

People from **France**, called the Normans, captured London in the Middle Ages. They built the Tower of London. Life in London was very hard. It was a **dirty** and **smelly** place, with lots of sickness.

Leonardo wants to tell you more!

1600s: This was a VERY bad time for London. Guy Fawkes tried to **blow up** the Houses of Parliament! There was a **civil war** and the king was **beheaded**! The **Great Plague** killed thousands of people, and **the Great Fire of London** destroyed nearly 80 percent of the city.

1700s: London grew more powerful and became an important **financial center.**

1800s: Under **Queen Victoria**, London got a lot bigger and became an important **industrial city**. But life for poor people was very bad.

Did you know?

The part of London where you'll find Buckingham Palace, the Houses of Parliament, London Zoo, and many other famous spots used to be a separate city called the **City of Westminster**!

Did you know?

People celebrate with fireworks and bonfires every year on the 5th of November—the day Guy Fawkes was arrested. **Guy Fawkes Day** was started to show thanks that he was captured!

Things to see only in London

There are **LOTS** of fantastic things to see in London!

The city combines old historic places with great modern spots. The streets are very busy, but you can also find large grassy **parks** where you can run and play. There are hundreds of **museums and art galleries, theme parks, zoos, old churches** ... and more!

London has many different **shops and markets,** and it is the home of one very special shop—**Hamleys Toy Store**. This magical place is the oldest toy store in the whole world!

You can see the **queen's main home** in London—**Buckingham Palace**. The dazzling **Crown Jewels** are also kept in London.

Did you know?

London is known for its special types of **guards** that protect important places. The guards at Buckingham Palace wear red and black uniforms with big black furry hats. The guards at the Tower of London are called **Beefeaters**, and they also wear a special uniform. You won't find these guards anywhere else in the UK!

Quizzes!

1. What is the oldest toy shop in the world called?

____

2. What people guard the Tower of London?

____

3. What is the monarch's main home called?

____

Answers: 1. Hamleys, 2. Beefeaters, 3. Buckingham Palace

Getting to and from London— by air and undersea!

Leonardo wants to tell you about some of the ways to get to and from London ... there are lots!

Planes

London has a whopping SIX main airports! The main airport is Heathrow. This is the biggest and busiest airport in the UK—and in all of Europe. It's also one of the busiest airports in the world! The other London airports are called Heathrow, Gatwick, Stansted, Luton, London City, and Southend.

Trains

Do you like trains? London is well connected to the rest of the UK by train. Some of the major train stations are called Euston, Victoria, Waterloo, King's Cross, St. Pancras, Liverpool Street, Charing Cross, and Paddington.

You can also get from London to many cities in Europe by train—on a railway that goes under the sea! The train is called the Eurostar, and it goes through the Channel Tunnel (a tunnel built under the English Channel). It's the longest undersea tunnel in the world!

Did you know?
When you combine all of its airports, London is the busiest city in the world for flights!

Did you know?
The Channel Tunnel's name is often shortened to just "the Chunnel"!

Have you ever heard of Paddington Bear?

Paddington Bear is a story character. He was sent to England from "deepest, darkest Peru," and he arrived at Paddington Station. That is how he got his name! He has many adventures, and he's very popular with children in the UK.

Paddington Bear located in Paddington Station

Getting around in London!

Buses

There are many buses that travel to different parts of London and beyond. Traditional London buses are very famous—they are bright red and have two levels. That's why they're called double-deckers.

Snap a picture of a red double-decker.

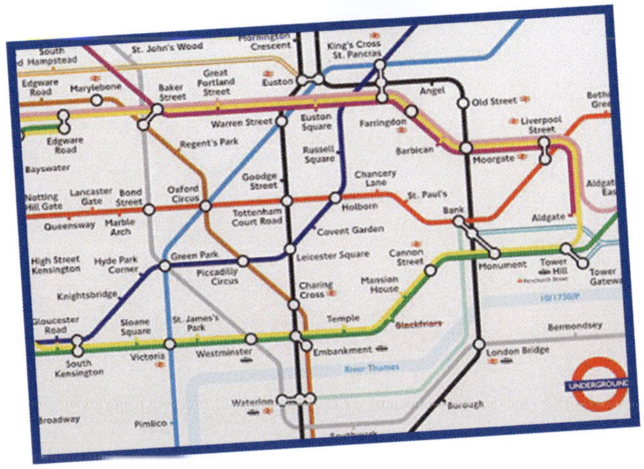

London Underground

The London Underground is a type of **fast subway system**. As the name shows, it runs underground! It connects almost all parts of the city, and it's one of the best ways to get between places. There are no traffic jams on the London Underground! 😉

There are many different lines (or routes) on the London Underground, and the maps look quite confusing! Once you get the hang of it though, it's actually very easy!

Taxis

There are regular taxis in London, just as you will find in almost every major city around the world. But London also has a special type of taxi—the big **black hackney cab**. These replaced horse-drawn carriages as a way to get around the city streets.

Did you know?
The nickname of the London Underground is **"the Tube"**!

What transportation have you used in London?

____

____

What is your favorite type of London transport?

____

Which of these is NOT a famous type of transport in London?

Answer: B is not a famous type of transportation in London.

Buckingham Palace:
Home of the Monarch!

Buckingham Palace was built in 1703, and it has been the official Royal home since the 1830s.

It is a grand and elegant building that is surrounded by a metal fence. Even by just peeking through the fence you can see how marvelous it is!

How many words can you make from "Buckingham Palace"?
For example: "ice"

____

____

____

Changing of the Guard

The palace is protected by Royal Guards. Every few days, there is an elaborate ceremony where new guards march to the palace with a band! They swap places with the old guards, who can then go back to their base.

TIP!
Ask your parents to check the schedule for the Changing of the Guard, because it changes throughout the year.

Did you know?
There are 775 rooms inside Buckingham Palace! And there are 52 bedrooms for the Royal Family and their guests!

Did you know?

Queen Elizabeth II was famous for her Corgis. She owned more than 30 of them during her lifetime!

Quizzes!

1. Can you guess how many bathrooms are in the palace?

A. 18 B. 38 C. 78 D. 108

2. How many bedrooms do you think there are for the palace's staff?

A. 92 B. 114 C. 159 D. 188

Answers: 1. C, 2. D

The Tower of London—
a 900-year-old castle

The majestic Tower of London was built in **1066** by French Normans who captured London. It's surrounded by a **moat** and **high walls** for protection. Back then, the local people hated it!

Over the years, the tower has been used in many ways. It's been a **home for the Royals**—and a famous prison where two of King Henry VIII's wives were beheaded! It's also been a **mint** (place where money is made), a place to **store weapons**, and even a **zoo!**

Today, the tower is guarded by **Beefeaters,** and it is home to some big birds called **ravens.** It has lots of interesting displays. Leonardo recommends: Don't miss the sparkling **Crown Jewels**, with more than 23,000 glittering gems!

Did you know?
A superstition says there must always be at least six ravens at the Tower of London ... or it will fall down! How many ravens did you see?

Can you help Leonardo find all these words that are connected with the Tower of London?

- ☐ Castle
- ☐ Prison
- ☐ Zoo
- ☐ Jewels
- ☐ Raven
- ☐ Moat
- ☐ Walls
- ☐ Mint
- ☐ Home
- ☐ Beefeater

A	C	R	S	H	K	L	G	V	M
E	M	O	H	S	X	S	Z	I	C
N	N	M	A	L	T	O	N	I	N
O	E	O	A	L	O	T	O	N	B
S	V	A	C	A	S	T	L	E	A
I	A	T	A	W	R	K	A	P	I
R	R	E	T	A	E	F	E	E	B
P	N	A	L	J	E	W	E	L	S

Take a picture of a raven!

London's grand and gorgeous religious places

London is filled with beautiful old churches and other religious buildings. Because of its many different cultures, London also has mosques, Hindu temples, Buddhist temples, synagogues, gurdwaras,* and more!

**Gurdwaras are Sikh (seek) temples. Sikhism began in India. It's the fifth most popular religion in the world.*

Two of the most famous religious buildings are Westminster Abbey and St. Paul's Cathedral. Both are very popular places for tourists to visit.

Westminster Abbey

This was built in the 1240s, but there had been a church at that same place for many years before.

The building has lots of beautiful details inside and outside. When you go inside, you can also visit the museum and see lots of religious art.

Westminster Abbey is the traditional place where new kings and queens are crowned. It's also where members of the Royal Family are buried when they die. Lots of Royal weddings have been held here. It's where Queen Elizabeth married her husband, Prince Philip (although she wasn't yet queen then). And it's where her grandson, Prince William, married Kate Middleton in 2011.

Did you know?

Eighty-eight churches burned down in the Great Fire of London. Many more were damaged or destroyed during the Reformation (a time when there was lots of fighting within the Christian church). And lots of London churches were also destroyed by bombs during World War II.

St. Paul's Cathedral

This enormous cathedral was built in the 1700s, after the previous church burned down. It stands at the highest point in London, and there has been a church here for more than 1,400 years.

St. Paul's has a beautiful dome on top. Inside, you'll find lots of pretty artwork, statues, and carvings. Many funerals of famous people have taken place here, as well as some Royal weddings.

More stunning sights!

There are many interesting and beautiful landmarks around London. Some are very old and some are quite modern—but all are great places to see when you're in London!

Leonardo wants to tell you about some of his favorites:

The Houses of Parliament

British lawmakers meet in the Houses of Parliament. This is a really long building that **sits next to the River Thames**. Leonardo likes all the spiky spires and the really tall clock tower.

Tower Bridge

Built in the late 1800s, the beautiful Tower Bridge crosses the River Thames. There are two parts to the bridge—the bottom part can **lift up to let tall boats go through**. You can walk across the top part and enjoy amazing views!

The Gherkin

This is one of London's most unusual modern buildings—and one of the **city's tallest buildings**. It opened in 2004. Can you see why it got the nickname "the Gherkin"? It looks like a giant pickle!

Did you know?

Many people think Big Ben is the name of the large clock tower next to the Houses of Parliament. But Big Ben is actually the name of the **main bell in the tower.** Listen to hear it chime every hour!

What is your favorite London landmark?

____

Why do you like it? What makes it special?

____

____

What are some of the main landmarks in your town or city?

____

____

So much to see at Trafalgar Square

Trafalgar Square is a big public square in the heart of London. It's a great place to get lots of beautiful pictures!

The square is surrounded by amazing **buildings**, such as the Admiralty Arch, the National Gallery, and St. Martin-in-the-Fields Church. There are interesting **statues**, **fountains**, and **monuments** in the square.

Did you know?
It's against the law to feed the pigeons in Trafalgar Square.

1. Walk to the middle of the square. There is a big statue. Do you know his name?

____

2. What does the man have on his head?

____

3. How many bronze lions are around the bottom?

____

4. What is the man holding in his left hand?

____

Answers: 1. Admiral/Lord Nelson, 2. Hat, 3. Four, 4. Sword

Other statues show important people in the British Navy's past and two old kings. One of the kings is sitting on a horse.

Did you know?
The person who designed the fountains at the bottom of the big statue also designed a lot of the buildings in India's capital city, New Delhi.

Can you help Leonardo to unscramble these words connected with Trafalgar Square?

Nlsnoe ____________________

Lonis ____________________

Ssuatet ____________________

Pengsio ____________________

Fntiosnua ____________________

Answers:
Nelson
Lions
Statues
Pigeons
Fountains

London's excellent ZOO!

London Zoo is home to LOADS of different cute and interesting animals. Take a stroll through the African zone and see animals like zebras, giraffes, and wild dogs. Wander through the rainforest area and spot lots of creatures in the daylight ... and then in the dark!

You can see the world's largest type of lizard, the fearsome-looking Komodo dragon. Come face-to-face with lions, tigers, penguins, hippos, monkeys, and gorillas—and have fun in the aquarium, the bug house, and the butterfly palace.

There is even a children's zone where you can get up close and friendly with animals like sheep, goats, pigs, and donkeys.

Leonardo recommends trying to make it to the animals' different feeding times.

Did you know?
London Zoo is the oldest scientific zoo in the world! The zoo was only for scientific study at first—but it opened to the public in 1847.

Leonardo loves penguins.
What is your favorite zoo animal?

____

Can you draw your favorite zoo animal?

TIP!
Tell your parents how they can save money AND avoid the long lines (or queues). Just buy London Zoo tickets online before your family visits!

More fun with animals!

If you love animals there are plenty of other places in London to make you smile ... 🙂

Mudchute Park and Farm

Here you can pet different animals in the petting zoo, feed the ducks, see lots of farm animals in the fields, and ride horses.

Battersea Park Children's Zoo

Leonardo thinks you will LOVE this zoo! It was designed **especially for kids,** and it specializes in smaller animals. There are lemurs, rabbits, pigs, birds, goats, ponies ... and more! There is also a fun play area with lots of **activities and rides.**

Sea Life London Aquarium

This is one of the biggest collections of **fascinating sea creatures** in all of Europe! You can see plenty of creatures from the ocean deep. And there are touch pools where you can find out what some of them actually feel like! (Soft? Sharp? Squishy?) 😮

Can you help Leonardo find these creatures in the word search?

One animal is missing—which one? ____________________

- ☐ Elephant
- ☐ Giraffe
- ☐ Horse
- ☐ Sheep
- ☐ Lion
- ☐ Cow
- ☐ Dog
- ☐ Goat
- ☐ Otter
- ☐ Rabbit
- ☐ Bear
- ☐ Cat
- ☐ Zebra
- ☐ Monkey
- ☐ Deer
- ☐ Bird
- ☐ Tiger
- ☐ Lizard
- ☐ Fish
- ☐ Snake

A	R	B	E	Z	I	G	T	N	C	P	F	A
N	A	I	R	T	E	I	J	A	M	E	I	G
Y	E	R	A	K	N	R	W	O	C	E	S	O
E	B	D	A	N	A	A	O	N	U	H	H	D
K	I	N	A	B	Y	F	H	O	R	S	E	F
N	S	E	B	L	H	F	A	P	I	D	S	L
O	T	I	G	E	R	E	G	I	E	S	O	I
M	T	L	I	Z	A	R	D	E	H	L	I	O
C	H	T	A	O	G	N	R	T	D	E	E	N

Answer: The Otter!

Thrilling theme parks

If you like fun, rides, and laughter galore, you'll LOVE London's different theme parks! These are Leonardo's favorites:

The Making of Harry Potter

Whether you loved the Harry Potter books and movies, or you just love all things magical, the Making of Harry Potter tour is **sure to be spell-binding fun!**

You can stand on the famous train platform and have your **picture taken** with the Hogwarts Express, **see robotic creatures from the movies**, gaze at the **spectacular sets**, spot numerous props, and **learn more** about how the popular Harry Potter films were made.

Did you know?
Madame Tussaud was born in France. Her name before she got married was Marie Grosholtz. She made her **first wax figure in 1777!** Some of her original models can still be seen at Madame Tussauds today.

Chessington World of Adventures

This super theme park has more than 40 different rides that will be fun for all your family! There is also a zoo that's packed with many different types of animals and a brilliant aquarium. Plus you'll find plenty of places for your family to stop for a bite to eat or a drink.

Madame Tussauds

Do you want to stand next to all your **favorite movie stars, pop singers,** and **famous athletes?** Perhaps there's a superhero or two that you're crazy about. Maybe you'd like to get close to world leaders, royalty, and well-known faces from the past.

Madame Tussauds has loads of different **lifelike wax models** to amaze you. And that's not all! There is a **fun ride and a thrilling 4D movie theatre**—and a chance to learn more about making the wax figures.

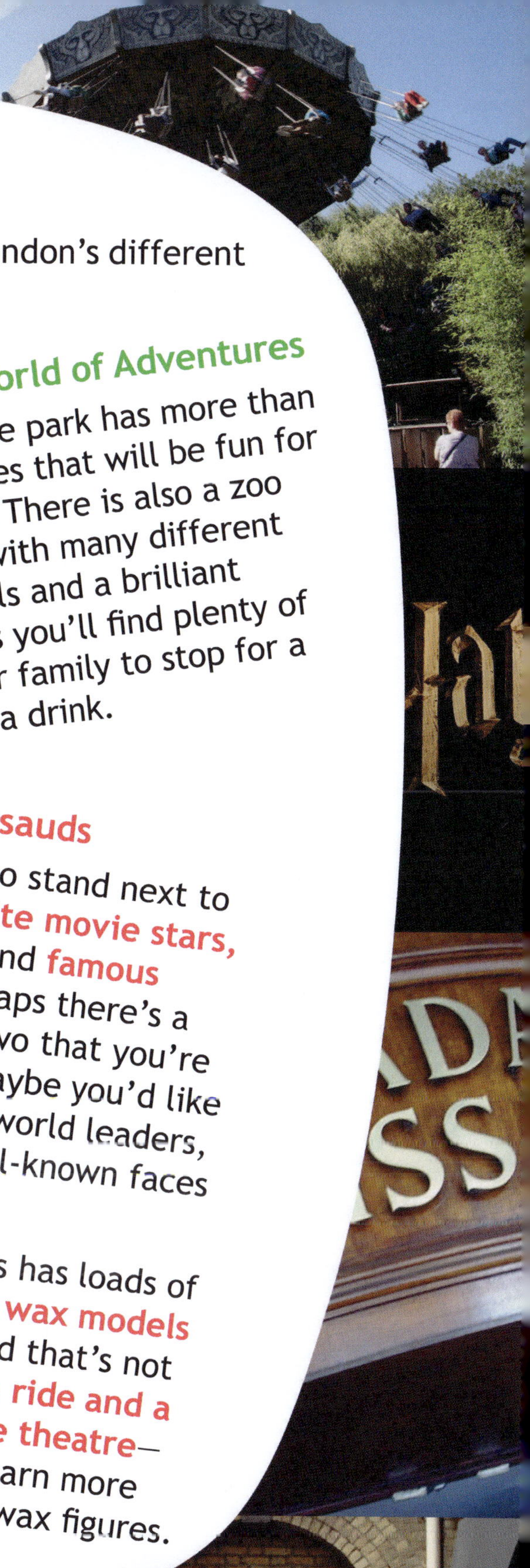

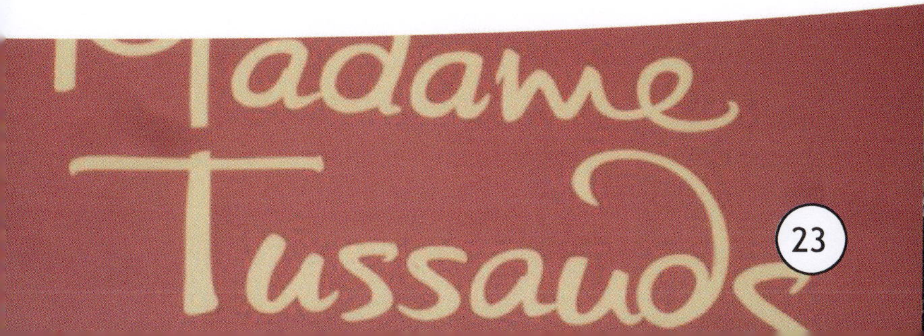

MORE fab theme parks!

Legoland Windsor

Do you like Legos? 🙂 Imagine a place full of things built entirely from Legos! At Legoland Windsor you can feast your eyes on **Lego sculptures** big and small ... They're sure to give you lots of ideas for your own Lego projects! **Miniland is especially fab!** Join one of the building workshops and see what you can **build yourself with Lego blocks.**

There are fun rides too. Many of them let you hop in the driver's seat and drive yourself around! Leonardo thinks you'll really enjoy the **great shows and the indoor water-play area.** There are lots of places to eat and drink around the park too. It's a really excellent day out!

Wet 'n' Wild at Waterfront Leisure Centre

This is a perfect place if you and your family want to **swim** and have tons of **fun in the water.**

Along with a regular swimming pool (for serious swimmers!) and leisure pools (where you can splash and play!!), there is a cool **wave machine**, an **erupting volcano**, a **waterfall**, **water jets**, and **inflatable toys**. Race your family to the bottom of the five-lane water slide! If you love speed, the Anaconda flume will be right up your alley!

Can you unscramble these things that you will find at Legoland or Wet 'n' Wild?

Rdise	R _ _ e _
Sileds	_ l _ _ e _
Ssohw	_ h _ _ _
Lgoe	L _ _ _
Splursectu	_ _ u _ _ _ u _ _ s

Answers: Rides, Slides, Shows, Lego, Sculptures

What was your favorite London theme park?

____

What ride did you like the best?

____

What other theme parks have you visited in other places?

____

____

A spooky look at London's past

There are a few places in London that offer lots of **spooky fun**.
Be warned though—they can be quite scary!

If you like **heart-pounding adventures**, Leonardo recommends these places for you and your family:

The London Dungeon

Go underground into the murky and **scary depths** of olden-day London. **Be terrified** by some of the city's famous criminals (played by very convincing actors)! The amazing sets and scenery, brilliant special effects, and different sights, sounds, and smells will give you a spine-tingling experience!

There are a few thrilling rides too, and many gory and funny tales to captivate and horrify you!

The London Bridge Experience

Go under the famous bridge and giggle and squeal your way through **London's murky past**. You can see how Queen Boudica battled with the Romans or experience the devastation of the Great Fire of London. **Come face-to-face with notorious criminals**, wander along medieval streets ... and more!

And all that's before you even enter the Tombs! Here, actors wait to give you chilling surprises, and the horrifying sets are designed to give you the creeps!

TIP!

The London Dungeon is designed to be scary fun. If you get really afraid, remember that **they are only actors!** Your parents can also ask one of the actors to lead you outside for a bit. So don't worry!

Looking out from the London Eye

The London Eye is a large **observation wheel** that lets you see far and wide across London. It is a great way to see lots of the famous city sights from above.

Take to the skies in one of the **glass capsules**, and soak up the many wonderful views. The wheel moves slowly, giving you lots of time to spot things and take plenty of pictures!

Did you know?

Leonardo wants to share some interesting facts about the London Eye with you:

- It is a towering 135 meters (443 feet) tall!
- In clear weather you can see for about 40 kilometers (25 miles) in every direction.
- It moves twice as fast as a tortoise sprinting! (That's pretty slow!)
- It took seven years to build!

Take a picture of the stunning London views.

Check off these famous places as you spot them from the London Eye:

- ☐ The Houses of Parliament
- ☐ The River Thames
- ☐ Buckingham Palace
- ☐ The Tower of London
- ☐ Tower Bridge
- ☐ The Gherkin
- ☐ London Zoo
- ☐ St Paul's Cathedral
- ☐ The Oval Cricket Ground
- ☐ Trafalgar Square
- ☐ Hyde Park
- ☐ Westminster Abbey

Time for a break ... parks, gardens, and play areas

There are lots of places around London where you can run and play, take some time out, and escape from the hurry of city life.

Leonardo likes to unwind in the many different parks, gardens, and play areas all around the city. He wants to tell you about some of his favorites:

Hyde Park

It's one of the biggest parks in London, and has the oldest boating lake in the city.

You can take a boat trip, relax by the water, or feed the ducks and swans that glide around the lake. If the weather is warm, head to the Joy of Life Fountain, where you can splash around in the water yourself!

You'll have lots of fun at the jungle play area too!

Did you know?
Hyde Park is about the same size as the old City of London!

St James's Park

There are lots of birds on the large lake, including big and greedy pelicans! You can watch the pelicans being fed every day at 2:30 p.m.

Cross the bridge to get nice views of the park and the palace.

Here's a duck for you to color. "Quack, quack!"

More places to run around and have heaps of fun!

Regent's Park

There are so many ways to have a great time here! Choose from several playgrounds, a boating lake, a sandpit, tree houses, tennis courts, cafes, vans and stands selling ice cream, and nature galore! What more could you want in a park?!

In the summer months, there are usually many outdoor festivals and live music too.

Richmond Park

If you like Bambi, you'll love seeing all the deer roaming freely in this huge park. It is the biggest of all the Royal Parks, and it has many beautiful plants and flowers to admire. There's a grand old mansion in the park too.

Did you know?

There are eight Royal Parks in London. In the olden days only members of the Royal Family and their guests were allowed to visit them. Now the beautiful green spaces and nature are open to everyone!

Check off these things as you see them in the parks:

☐ Duck	☐ Flower
☐ Swan	☐ Ice cream
☐ Flying bird	☐ Football
☐ Boat	☐ Umbrella
☐ Butterfly	☐ Squirrel
☐ Beetle	☐ Frisbee

What's your favorite color of flower?

____

Make this pretty flower your favorite color.

Even more outdoor fun!

Holland Park

A great place for adventure! Holland Park has loads of stuff for climbing, a tire swing, an exciting zip line, and a giant seesaw! You can see lots of big fish in the pond, as well as pretty Japanese gardens, a waterfall, and an old mansion.

TIP!

Ask your parents to pack a picnic when you go to a park, so you can sit on the grass and enjoy an outdoor lunch!

Do you go to the park a lot at home?

____

What are your favorite things to play on in the park?

____

Which London parks did you visit?

____

____

What was your favorite London park?

____

Complete these things Leonardo likes to play on and play with when he goes to different parks:

S _ _ n _

S _ e _ _ w

S l _ d _

F _ i _ _ e _

F _ _ t _ a _ l

F _ _ e n _ s

C _ r _ u _ _ l

Answers: Swing, Seesaw, Slide, Frisbee, Football, Friends, Carousel

FIND SOME SOUVENIRS ...

Shopping in London

London has lots of exciting places for **shopping**. If you and your family are looking for interesting **souvenirs**, **fabulous new clothes**, **gifts to take back for friends and family,** pretty things for your house, and more, you'll find lots of choices in London!

There are huge department stores, lively markets, and everything else in between.

London's main shopping areas are known for different things.

Where would you most like to shop?

- **Oxford Street:** Lots of well-known brands.
- **Bond Street:** Expensive and luxurious!
- **Knightsbridge:** Famous, fashionable, and fancy.
- **Covent Garden:** Cute boutiques, a funky market, and a Punch and Judy puppet show!
- **Carnaby Street:** Far-out fashion and lots of places to eat!
- **Piccadilly:** Great shops surrounded by history and culture.

What do you want to buy in London?

What is your favorite London shopping place?

What is the most interesting souvenir you've spied in London?

Did you know?
Harrods is one of the most famous department stores in the city. It opened in 1824, and it was the first place in England to have an **escalator**! It is also the **biggest** store in the UK.

PART 2

Shopping in London

Did you know?

Carnaby Street has been a trendy and popular part of London for many years. It is known for its unusual and independent shops, where you can find some really unique and interesting things.

It was one of the coolest parts of London in the 1960s and 1970s. Lots of famous bands and music stars used to hang out here.
Today, it still has a completely different vibe than other parts of London.

Did you know?

Selfridges is the biggest department store on Oxford Street, and it's the second biggest store in the UK. It was the first place in the world where TV was shown to the public!

How many words can you make from Carnaby Street?
For example: "Can"

____

____

____

If you look above the main entrance, there is a statue of the Queen of Time.

1. What color is her dress? ____________________
2. What does she have behind her head? ____________________
3. How many mermen* are kneeling by her feet? __________
4. What is she holding in her hand? ____________________

**Merman: Half-man, half fish*

Answers: 1. Blue and gray; 2. Clock; 3. Two; 4. A ball (with an angel-like figure on it)

Did you know?

Do you like toys? Hamleys, the oldest toy shop in the world, first opened in 1760! Back then, it was called Noah's Ark. There are more than 50,000 toys and games inside, and you can play with lots of them in the shop!

200-plus terrific museums!

How many museums do you think there are in London?
More than 240 in all!!! 🙂

There are museums for almost every interest, but Leonardo thinks these are some of the best ones for you and your family:

Horniman Museum

How would you like to come face-to-face with **a giant walrus** ... or see busy bees at work ... or watch beautiful fish? Maybe you'd like to try playing some interesting musical instruments, see lots of artwork, or walk along amazing nature trails?

These are just a few of the cool things waiting for you at the excellent Horniman Museum! **This is one of the best museums in London for kids!**

There are many different, fascinating displays and lots of hands-on activities for you to try!

You can learn more about nature and people, and the large gardens are great for running and playing.

Mark on the scale how cool this museum was:

List your favorite things you saw and did at the Horniman Museum:

____

____

____

____

LONDON'S MUSEUMS ...

Pirates, mummies, and more !

The Golden Hinde

Do you love pirate stories and the big blue sea? Then step aboard the *Golden Hinde*, matey, and tread the boards of one of the first ships to ever sail all around the world!

There's so much to see and do on this huge reconstructed warship. Leonardo thinks you'll be shouting, "Ahoy there!" in no time at all!

British Museum

Would you like to learn more about ancient Egypt and see a real mummy? What about going back into the mighty Roman Empire or ancient Greece? You can take a journey all around the world—and go through all different time periods—at the fantastic British Museum.

There are hundreds of exciting items and many different displays in the museum's whopping 90-plus rooms!

Did you know?
"Hinde" is the name for a female deer!

Circle the things that are connected with pirates:

CINEMAS
PARROTS
DESERT ISLAND
SHIPS
ANCHOR
SUNGLASSES
ICE CREAM
CARS
HORSE
TREASURE
EYE PATCH

TIP!
Pick up an activity backpack at the British Museum. It will give you lots of fun things to do as you visit the different displays.

Answers: Desert Island, Ships, Parrots, Eye Patch, Anchor, Treasure

A museum for toys and games!

Young V&A Museum

If you love toys and games, then this hands-on museum is for you!

You can look at lots of **interesting old toys** and see **how kids played in the past**—and check out newer toys too. And there are plenty for you to play with yourself! You can also sit and listen to an **exciting story**, go on **a treasure hunt**, challenge your family to different board games, **ride a rocking horse** ... and more!

Did you know?

The initials **V & A** stand for Victoria and Albert.

Do you know who they were?

____

____

Answer: Queen Victoria and her husband, Prince Albert.

What museums did you visit in London?

____

____

What was your favorite London museum?

____

What things did you like seeing in the museums?

____

____

____

London theaters and shows you're sure to enjoy ...

The West End is the heart of the London theater scene, where you'll find lots of terrific shows, musicals, and performances. There are many more theaters around the city too, so get ready to be entertained!

Your family will be able to enjoy some excellent shows that are great for all ages!

Leonardo thinks these are especially fab:

Puppet Theatre Barge

Do you like puppets? How about boats? Why not combine the two? Watch a spectacular puppet show as you bob on the River Thames! You and your family can see lots of exciting stories acted out by the beautiful puppets on strings.

Have you ever seen a musical before?

____

Have you seen a play before?

____

What shows would you like to see in London?

____

____

Unicorn Theatre

Close to London Bridge, the Unicorn has two great theaters with lots of performances especially for kids. There are also great workshops where you can practice your own acting skills.

Polka Theatre

There's lots to do at this fantastic children's theater. You can watch an entertaining show, join a workshop, have fun in the play area, see interesting displays, and meet other kids!

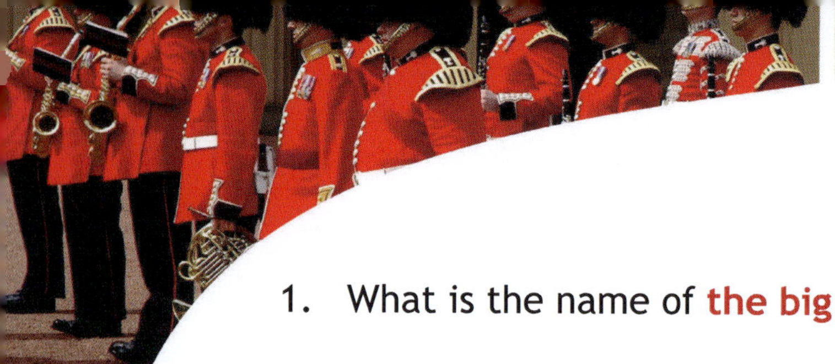

London trivia

1. What is the name of **the big observation wheel** in London? ____________________
2. Where are the **Crown Jewels kept?** ____________________
3. Where can you see the **Changing of the Guard Ceremony?** ____________________
4. What should you **not feed** in Trafalgar Square? ____________________
5. Does **Hamleys** sell animals, clothes, toys, or books? ____________________
6. What is the name of **London's big domed cathedral?** ____________________
7. What is **Big Ben?** ____________________
8. What is the nickname of the **London Underground?** ____________________
9. What's the nickname of the **tall, vegetable-like modern building?** ____________________
10. What color are traditional **London taxis?** ____________________
11. Where can you have fun with **Lego?** ____________________
12. In which park can you see **lots of deer?** ____________________
13. What museum has a **giant walrus?** ____________________
14. What is the name of **London's River**? ____________________
15. What's the **biggest store** in the UK? ____________________

Answers: 1. London Eye, 2. Tower of London, 3. Buckingham Palace, 4. Pigeons, 5. Toys, 6. St. Paul's, 7. Bell, 8. The Tube, 9. Gherkin, 10. Black, 11. Legoland, 12. Richmond Park, 13. Horniman, 14. Thames, 15. Harrods

London fun and facts

Have you heard the popular children's song *"London Bridge Is Falling Down"*? Can you sing it? London Bridge has been rebuilt many times over the years. It's a sturdy bridge now, but long ago, parts of an earlier bridge really did fall down!

Have you noticed what color traditional phone booths and mailboxes are in London? (Clue: They are the same color as the traditional buses!)

____

Did you also see what symbol is on both?

____

Color the phone box!

Answers: Red; A crown

Did you know?
The nickname for a person from London is a "Cockney."

Did you know?
Policemen in London (and the UK) are nicknamed "bobbies"!

Can you find eight differences between these crowns?

Here's a bobby hat ... Can you draw your own face under the hat?

Code breaker

Can you crack the code?! Use the key to figure out Leonardo's action-packed journal entry about his trip to London:

A = X, E = Q, O = J, N = 2, D = 5, R = 7, S = 9, P = *, T = #, L = %

People say if you're tired of %J25J2 (_ _ _ _ _ _) then you're tired of life. I really don't know how anyone could be tired of %J25J2 (_ _ _ _ _ _)! There are so many great things to 9QQ (_ _ _) and do. I loved it!!

I spent hours looking at all the incredible toys in HXM%QY9 (_ _ _ _ _ _ _) and a whole day watching different animals at %J25J2 ZJJ (_ _ _ _ _ _ _ _ _). Chessington World of Adventures was ace! I felt a bit scared in the %J25J2 5U2GQJ2 (_ _ _ _ _ _ _ _ _ _ _ _ _), but it was really cool! Madame #U99XU59 (_ _ _ _ _ _ _ _) was good too, and we went to lots of excellent MU9QUM9 (_ _ _ _ _ _ _). I liked the views from the %J25J2 QYQ (_ _ _ _ _ _ _ _ _).

2Q%9J2'9 (_ _ _ _ _ _'_) Column in Trafalgar Square is really tall and BUCKI2GHXM *X%XCQ (_ _ _ _ _ _ _ _ _ _ _ _ _ _ _ _ _) is really grand—I would love to live somewhere like that! I really enjoyed seeing the Changing of the Guard Ceremony—the BX25 (_ _ _ _) and soldiers were fab! I took so many pictures at the #JWQ7 of %J25J2 (_ _ _ _ _ of _ _ _ _ _ _) and of #JWQ7 B7I5GQ (_ _ _ _ _ _ _ _ _ _ _). The city is really busy so it was nice to spend some time in HY5Q *X7K (_ _ _ _ _ _ _ _) and Regent's Park.

We got around a lot using the #UBQ (_ _ _ _). I tried a traditional roast dinner too—it was yummy! I really did love London—when can I go again?!

Can you unscramble these famous London places?

1. Hsueso fo Petlramnai

____

2. Wmisteretns Aebyb

____

3. heT Ldonno Eey

____

4. Twroe Bdregi

____

5. Bingmachuk Placae

____

6. Lnondo ooZ

____

Answers: 1. Houses of Parliament, 2. Westminster Abbey, 3. The London Eye, 4. Tower Bridge, 5. Buckingham Palace, 6. London Zoo

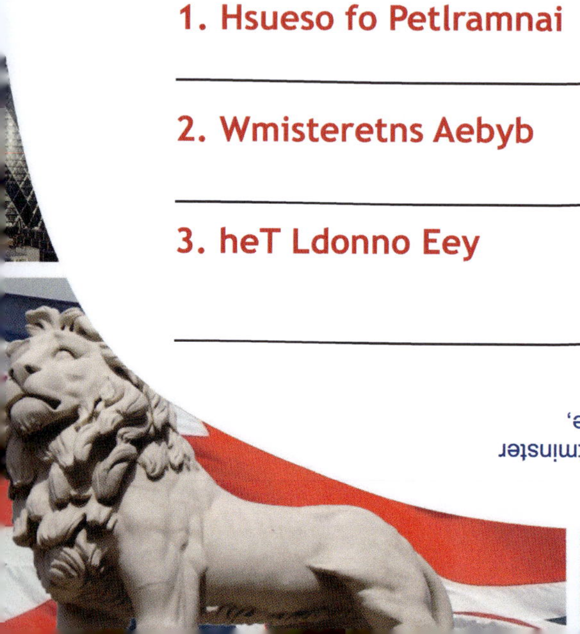

Summary of the trip

We had great fun, what a pity it is over ...

Whom did we meet ...

Did you meet tourists from other countries? Yes/No

If you did meet tourists, where did they come from? (Name their nationalities):

Shopping and souvenirs ...

What did you buy on the trip?

What did you want to buy, but ended up not buying?

Experiences

What are the most memorable experiences of the trip?

Rating the trip: Our favorite things

Grade the most beautiful places and the best experiences of your journey:

First Place

Second Place

Third Place

And now, a difficult task—discuss it with your family and decide ...

What did you enjoy most on the trip?

RECORD YOUR ADVENTURES!

My Journal

Date	What did we do?

RECORD YOUR ADVENTURES!

My Journal

Date	What did we do?

RECORD YOUR ADVENTURES!

My Journal

Acknowledgments

Key: t=top, b=bottom, l=left, r=right, c=center; m=main image; bg=background

All images are from **ShutterStock or public domain except those mentioned.**

Attributions: 13br-By Jin Zan (Own work) [CC BY-SA 3.0 (http://creativecommons.org/licenses/by-sa/3.0)], via Wikimedia Commons; 13ml-Lewis Clarke [CC BY-SA 2.0 (http://creativecommons.org/licenses/by-sa/2.0)], via Wikimedia Commons; 14m-By Sunil060902 (Own work) [CC BY-SA 3.0 (http://creativecommons.org/licenses/by-sa/3.0) or GFDL (http://www.gnu.org/copyleft/fdl.html)], via Wikimedia Commons; 17m-By Georgios Pazios (Alaniaris) (Έργο αυτού που το ανεβάζει (own work)) [Attribution], via Wikimedia Commons; 17br-CherryX per Wikimedia Commons [CC BY-SA 3.0 (http://creativecommons.org/licenses/by-sa/3.0)], via Wikimedia Commons; 23tr-By Chris Sampson (Flickr: 310812-012 CPS) [CC BY 2.0 (http://creativecommons.org/licenses/by/2.0)], via Wikimedia Commons; 24tl-By Rob Young profile (Flickr) [CC BY 2.0 (http://creativecommons.org/licenses/by/2.0)], via Wikimedia Commons; 24bl-Alex McGregor [CC BY-SA 2.0 (http://creativecommons.org/licenses/by-sa/2.0)], via Wikimedia Commons; 25mt-By Gripweed (Own work) [CC BY-SA 3.0 (http://creativecommons.org/licenses/by-sa/3.0)], via Wikimedia Commons; 25br-www.CGPGrey.com [CC BY 3.0 (http://creativecommons.org/licenses/by/3.0)], via Wikimedia Commons; 25mb-By Duncan Harris from Nottingham, UK (London Dungeon) [CC BY 2.0 (http://creativecommons.org/licenses/by/2.0)], via Wikimedia Commons, 25tr-Photograph by Mike Peel (www.mikepeel.net). [CC BY-SA 4.0 (http://creativecommons.org/licenses/by-sa/4.0)], via Wikimedia Commons; 31mtr-DearCatastropheWaitress at en.wikipedia [GFDL (http://www.gnu.org/copyleft/fdl.html), CC-BY-SA-3.0 (http://creativecommons.org/licenses/by-sa/3.0/) or CC BY 2.5 (http://creativecommons.org/licenses/by/2.5)], from Wikimedia Commons; 31mb-By Chmee2 (Own work) [CC BY-SA 3.0 (http://creativecommons.org/licenses/by-sa/3.0)], via Wikimedia Commons; 32mt-By Fæ (Self-photographed) [CC BY-SA 3.0 (http://creativecommons.org/licenses/by-sa/3.0)], via Wikimedia Commons; 32mb-PAUL FARMER [CC BY-SA 2.0 (http://creativecommons.org/licenses/by-sa/2.0)], via Wikimedia Commons, 33bl-By (□□ □□□□Own work) [CC BY-SA 4.0 (http://creativecommons.org/licenses/by-sa/4.0)], via Wikimedia Commons; 34mt-David Hawgood [CC BY-SA 2.0 (http://creativecommons.org/licenses/by-sa/2.0)], via Wikimedia Commons; 34bl-By Sascha Pohflepp (Flickr: V&A museum of childhood) [CC BY 2.0 (http://creativecommons.org/licenses/by/2.0)], via Wikimedia Commons; 34mb-By Scott Wylie [CC BY 2.0 (http://creativecommons.org/licenses/by/2.0)], via Wikimedia Commons; 34bl-By Cristian Bortes from Cluj-Napoca, Romania (Childhood Museum - London - September 2008) [CC BY 2.0 (http://creativecommons.org/licenses/by/2.0)], via Wikimedia Commons; 34tr-By Cristian Bortes from Cluj-Napoca, Romania (Childhood Museum - London - September 2008) [CC BY 2.0 (http://creativecommons.org/licenses/by/2.0)], via Wikimedia Commons; 35mtr-By Unicorn Theatre (Own work) [CC BY-SA 3.0 (http://creativecommons.org/licenses/by-sa/3.0)], via Wikimedia Commons; 35br-By Stmike7 (Own work) [CC BY-SA 3.0 (http://creativecommons.org/licenses/by-sa/3.0)], via Wikimedia Commons, 35mcr-Phillip Perry [CC BY-SA 2.0 (http://creativecommons.org/licenses/by-sa/2.0)], via Wikimedia Commons.

ENJOY MORE FUN ADVENTURES WITH LEONARDO AND FlyingKids®

FOR FREE DOWNLOADS OF MORE ACTIVITIES, GO TO WWW.THEFLYINGKIDS.COM

Printed in Dunstable, United Kingdom

72382205R00027